This Body Is Made of Camphor
and Gopherwood

OTHER BOOKS BY ROBERT BLY

Poetry

SILENCE IN THE SNOWY FIELDS

THE LIGHT AROUND THE BODY

THE TEETH MOTHER NAKED AT LAST

JUMPING OUT OF BED

SLEEPERS JOINING HANDS

OLD MAN RUBBING HIS EYES

THE MORNING GLORY

Translations (*Poetry*)

TWENTY POEMS OF GEORG TRAKL
  (WITH JAMES WRIGHT)

NERUDA AND VALLEJO: SELECTED POEMS
  (WITH JAMES WRIGHT AND JOHN KNOEPFLE)

LORCA AND JIMÉNEZ: SELECTED POEMS

FRIENDS, YOU DRANK SOME DARKNESS.
  *MARTINSON, EKELÖF AND TRANSTRÖMER:
  SELECTED POEMS*

RILKE: TEN SONNETS TO ORPHEUS

THE KABIR BOOK: *44 OF THE ECSTATIC POEMS OF KABIR*

Translations *(Fiction)*

HUNGER, *BY KNUT HAMSUN*

THE STORY OF GÖSTA BERLING, *BY SELMA LAGERLÖF*

Interviews

TALKING ALL MORNING: *COLLECTED INTERVIEWS
  AND CONVERSATIONS* (FALL, 1977)

This Body Is Made of Camphor and Gopherwood

Prose Poems by
ROBERT BLY

Drawings by
GENDRON JENSEN

HARPER & ROW, PUBLISHERS
NEW YORK, HAGERSTOWN, SAN FRANCISCO, LONDON

We are grateful to the editors of the following magazines in whose pages some of these poems have been printed:

Field, The North Stone Review, Choice, The Iowa Review, Boundary 2, The Chariton Review, The Seneca Review, James Scrimgeour's *What Is That Country Standing Inside You, Montana Gothic, The American Poetry Review,* and *Paris Review.*

FIRST EDITION

Designed by Gloria Adelson

ISBN 0–06–010363–9

ISBN 0–06–010414–7 (pbk.)

LIBRARY OF CONGRESS CATALOG CARD NUMBER: 76–47258

77 78 79 80 81 10 9 8 7 6 5 4 3 2 1

Gendron would like to dedicate this book to:
"All the waters of this world"

Contents

This Body Is Made of Camphor
and Gopherwood

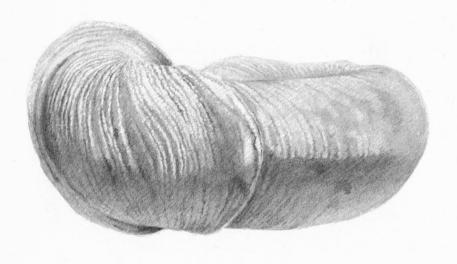

Walking Swiftly

When I wake, I hear sheep eating apple peels just outside
the screen. The trees are heavy, soaked, cold and hushed, the
sun just rising. All seems calm, and yet somewhere inside I
am not calm. We live in wooden buildings made of
two-by-fours, making the landscape nervous for a hundred
miles. And the Emperor when he was sixty called for
rhinoceros horn, for sky-blue phoenix eggs shaped from
veined rock, dipped in rooster blood. Around him the wasps
kept guard, the hens continued their patrol, the oysters open
and close all questions. The heat inside the human body
grows, it does not know where to throw itself—for a while it
knots into will, heavy, burning, sweet, then into generosity,
that longs to take on the burdens of others, then into mad
love that lasts forever. The artist walks swiftly to his studio,
and carves oceanic waves into the dragon's mane.

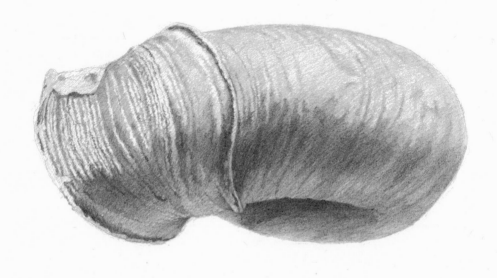

The Left Hand

My friend, this body is made of camphor and gopherwood.
Where it goes, we follow, even into the Ark. As the light
comes in sideways from the west over damp spring buds and
winter trash, the body comes out hesitatingly, and we are
shaken, we weep, how is it that we feel no one has ever
loved us? This protective lamplit left hand hovering over its
own shadow on the page seems more loved than we are. . . .
And when we step into a room where we expect to find
someone, we do not believe our eyes, we walk all the way
over the floor and feel the bed. . . .

The Sleeper

He came in and sat by my side, and I did not wake up. I
went on dreaming of vast houses with rooms I had not seen,
of men suddenly appearing whom I did not know, but who
knew me, of thistles whose points shone as if a light were
inside.

A man came to me and began to play music. One arm lay
outside the covers. He put the dulcimer in my hand but I did
not play it. I went on, hearing.

Why didn't I wake up? And why didn't I play? Because I
am asleep, and the sleeping man is all withdrawn into
himself. He thinks the sound of a shutting door is a tooth
falling from his head, or his head rolling on the ground.

Finding the Father

   This body offers to carry us for nothing—as the ocean
carries logs—so on some days the body wails with its great
energy, it smashes up the boulders, lifting small crabs, that
flow around the sides. Someone knocks on the door, we do
not have time to dress. He wants us to come with him
through the blowing and rainy streets, to the dark house. We
will go there, the body says, and there find the father whom
we have never met, who wandered in a snowstorm the night
we were born, who then lost his memory, and has lived since
longing for his child, whom he saw only once . . . while he
worked as a shoemaker, as a cattle herder in Australia, as a
restaurant cook who painted at night. When you light the
lamp you will see him. He sits there behind the door . . . the
eyebrows so heavy, the forehead so light . . . lonely in his
whole body, waiting for you.

Looking from Inside My Body

The sun sinking. Each minute the air darker. The night
thickens near the ground, pulls the earth down to it.

I look from inside my body. And if my body is earth, then
what? Then I am down here, thickening as night comes on.
And the moon will stay up there. Some part of me is up
there too. How far it is up to that part!

There are earth things, earthly, joined, they are snuggled
down in one manger, one sweep of arms holds them, one
clump of pine, the owlets sit together in one hollow tree. . . .

Night will come—and then what will happen? What has
been sun in me all day will drop underneath the earth, and
travel sizzling along the underneath-ocean-darkness path. . . .
There a hundred developed saints lie stretched out, throwing
bits of darkness onto the road. . . .

And later I will go inside, and lie down on my bed, and
suddenly my moon will vanish. The sleeper will go down
toward utter darkness. . . . Who will be with him? He will
meet another prisoner in the dungeon, alone with the baker.

The moon outside the bedroom will travel on alone over
the darkened earth all night, slipping through the arms
reached up to it. . . . It will go on, looking. . . .

Going Out to Check the Ewes

My friend, this body is food for the thousand dragons of
the air, each dragon light as a needle. This body loves us,
and carries us home from our hoeing.

It is ancient, and full of the bales of sleep. In its vibrations
the sun rolls along under the earth, the spouts over the ocean
curl into our stomach . . . water revolves, spouts seen by
skull eyes at mid-ocean, this body of herbs and gopherwood,
this blessing, this lone ridge patrolled by water. . . . I get up,
morning is here. The stars still out; the black winter sky
looms over the unborn lambs. The barn is cold before dawn,
the gates slow. . . .

This body longs for itself far out at sea, it floats in the
black heavens, it is a brilliant being, locked in the prison of
human dullness. . . .

Galloping Horses

The horses gallop east, over the steppes, each with its
rider, hard. Each rider carries a strip of red cloth raised
above his head. The horses leap over a line of fire. Then a
stream, they leap higher, hooves push into the mud. Then a
crevice—space stretched out sideways—a few horses fall in.
Now they meet their fourth obstacle—flesh. . . . It is a
Garden, elephant trunks reach lazily up into tree branches,
and the gazelles hurry over the plain like blood corpuscles in
a storm, flock on flock, even the monkeys have hair. And the
horses slow, they become confused among so many gentle
animals, the riders look to the side and behind them, turning
in their saddles to see the large animals peacefully grazing
behind.

A Dream of What Is Missing

Last night such glad powerful dreams, each tile laid down
of luminous glazed clay. . . . The dream said that The One
Who Sees the Whole does not have the senses, but the
longing for the senses. That longing is terrible, and terrifying
—the herd of gazelles running over the savannah—and
intense and divine, and I saw it lying over the dark floor . . .
in layers there. The one who thinks does not have feeling,
but the longing for feeling—that longing makes the lines of
force at the bottom of Joseph's well. In the dream I saw the
lumps of dirt that heal the humpbacked, what rolls slowly
upward from the water, and prowls around the rocky edges
of the desert, keeping the hermit inside his own chest. . . .

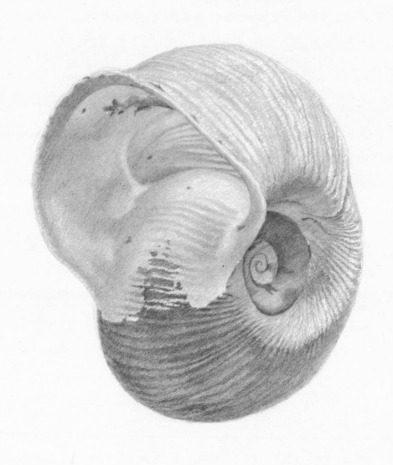

Falling into Holes in Our Sentences

This body holds its protective walls around us, it watches us whenever we walk out. Each step we take in conversation with our friends, moving slowly or flying, the body watches us, calling us into what is possible, into what is not said, into the shuckheap of ruined arrowheads, or the old man with two fingers gone.

We take our first step in words each day, and instantly fall into a hole in the sounds we make. Overly sane afternoons in a room during our twenties come back to us in the form of a son who is mad, every longing another person had that we failed to see the body returns to us as a squinting of the eyes when we talk, and no sentimentality, only the ruthless body performing its magic, transforming each of our confrontations into energy, changing our scholarly labors over white-haired books into certainty and healing power, and our cruelties into an old man with missing fingers.

We talk all morning of the confusion of others, and in daylight the car slides off the road, I give advice in public as if I were adult, that night in a dream I see a policeman holding a gun to the head of a frightened girl, who is blindfolded, we console each other, and opening a *National Geographic* see an old woman lying with her mouth open.

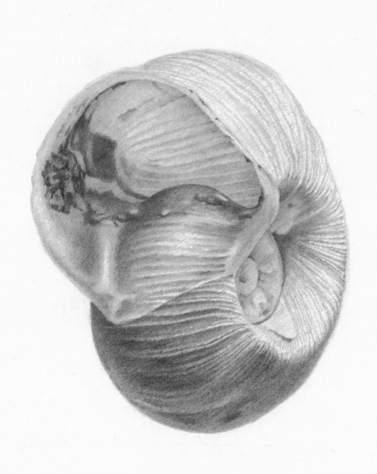

Walking to the Next Farm

It has been snowing all day. Three of us start out across
the fields. The boots sink in to the ankles, but go on; our feet
move through the most powerful snow energy. There is
falling snow above us, and below us, and on all sides. My
eyes feel wild, as if a new body were rising, with tremendous
swirls in its flow; its whirlpools move with their face upward,
as those whirls in the Missouri that draw in green
cottonwoods from collapsed earth banks, pull them down
with all their branches. And our feet carry the male energy
that disappears, as my brother's energy did, in its powerful
force field his whole life disappeared, and all the trees on his
farm went with it. . . .

There is some sort of energy that comes off the fierce
man's hair. It is not a halo, but a background of flames. The
energy increases, while "more and more docile men are
being born each day." As the Tibetan exhales, fifty pale men
melt back into the ground. Huns fade back into the forest
around Vienna, the doctor leaps up from his desk, he curses
the stupidity of his life, grinds his teeth. Lenin refuses to eat
with others. The carriage goes on through the night.

Then what is asked of us? To stop sacrificing one energy
for another. They are not different energies anyway, not
"male" or "female," but whirls of different speeds as they

revolve. We must learn to worship both, and give up the idea of one god. . . . I taste the snow, lying on a branch. It tastes slow. It is as slow as the whirl in the boulder lying beneath the riverbed. . . . Its swirls take nine thousand years to complete, but they too pull down the buffalo skin boats into their abysses, many souls with hair go down.

> The light settles down in front of each snowflake,
> and the dark rises up behind it,
> and inside its own center it lives!

The Origin of the Praise of God

for Lewis Thomas,
and his *The Lives of a Cell*

My friend, this body is made of bone and excited protozoa
. . . and it is with my body that I love the fields. How do I
know what I feel but what the body tells me? Erasmus
thinking in the snow, translators of Virgil who burn up the
whole room, the man in furs reading the Arabic astrologer
falls off his three-legged stool in astonishment—this is the
body, so beautifully carved inside, with the curves of the
inner ear, and the husk so rough, knuckle-brown.

As we walk we enter the magnetic fields of other bodies,
and every smell we take in the communities of protozoa see,
and a being inside leaps up toward it, as a horse rears at the
starting gate. When we come near each other, we are drawn
down into the sweetest pools of slowly circling energies,
slowly circling smells. And the protozoa know there are
odors the shape of oranges, of tornadoes, of octopuses. . . .

> The sunlight lays itself down before the protozoa,
> the night opens itself out behind it,
> and inside its own energy it lives!

So the space between two people diminishes, it grows less
and less, no one to weep, they merge at last. The sound that
pours from the fingertips awakens clouds of cells far inside

the body, and beings unknown to us start out in a pilgrimage
to their Saviour, to their holy place. Their holy place is a
small black stone, that they remember from Protozoic times,
when it was rolled away from a door . . . and it was after that
they found their friends, who helped them to digest the hard
grains of this world. . . . The cloud of cells awakens,
intensifies, swarms . . . the cells dance inside beams of
sunlight so thin we cannot see them. . . . To them each ray is
a vast palace, with thousands of rooms. From the dance of the
cells praise sentences rise to the throat of the man praying
and singing alone in his room. He lets his arms climb above
his head, and says, "Now do you still say you cannot choose
the Road?"

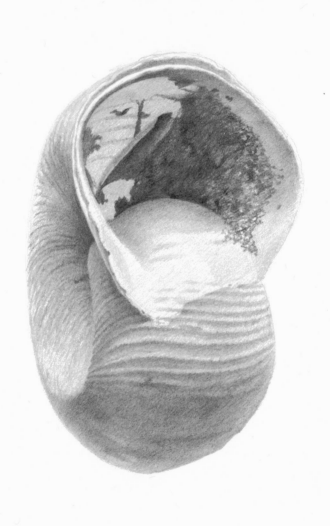

Coming In for Supper

It is lovely to follow paths in the snow made by human feet. The paths wind gaily around the ends of drifts, they rise and fall. How amazed I am, after working hard in the afternoon, that when I sit down at the table, with my elbows touching the elbows of my children, so much love flows out and around in circles. . . . The children have been working on a play.

Each child flares up as a small fire in the woods. . . . Biddy chortles over her new hair, curled for the first time last night, over her new joke song.

> *Yankee Doodle went to town,*
> *riding on a turtle,*
> *turned the corner just in time*
> *to see a lady's girdle. . . .*

Mary knows the inscription she wants on her coffin if she dies young, and says it:

> *Where the bee sucks there suck I*
> *In a cowslip's bell I lie. . . .*

She is obstinate and light at the same time, a heron who flies pulling long legs behind, or balances unsteadily on a stump, aware of all the small birds at the edge of the forest, where it is shadowy . . . longing to capture the horse with only one hair from its mane. . . .

Biddy can pick herself up and run over the muddy river bottom without sinking in; she already knows all about holding, and kisses each grownup carefully before going to bed; at the table she faces you laughing, bending over slightly toward you, like a tree bent in wind, protective of this old shed she is leaning over. . . .

And all the books around on the walls are feathers in a great feather bed, they weigh hardly anything! Only the encyclopedias, left lying on the floor near the chair, contain the heaviness of the three-million-year-old life of the oyster-shell breakers, those long dusks—they were a thousand years long then—that fell over the valley from the cave mouth (where we sit). . . . The inventions found, then lost again . . . the last man killed by flu who knew how to weave a pot of river clay the way the wasps do. . . . Now he is dead and only the wasps know in the long river-mud grief. The marmoset curls its toes once more around the slippery branch, remembering the furry chest of its mother, long since sunk into a hole that appeared in the afternoon. . . .

Dinner is finished, and the children pass out invitations composed with felt pens.

You are invited to "The Thwarting of Captain Alphonse"

PRINCESS GARDINER:	MARY BLY
CAPTAIN ALPHONSE:	WESLEY RAY
AUNT AUGUST:	BIDDY BLY
RAILWAY TRACK:	NOAH BLY
TRAIN:	SAM RAY

Costumes and Sets by Mary Bly and Wesley Ray
Free Will Offering Accepted

How the Ant Takes Part

Smoke rises from mountain depths, a girl walks by the water. This is the body of water near where we sleep. And the mountain climber picks his way up the rocky scrap. How far up on the mountainside he is! As he disappears over the pass, an ant in the village below hurries up his mound of dirt, a woman turns her face back to the stove. Her man at that instant feels some mistake in his heart. The girl moves her hands, all the images rearrange themselves, the bacteria go in swarms through the ocean-salted blood.

When the Wheel Does Not Move

There is a dense energy that pools in the abdomen and wants to move and does not! It lies there fierce and nomadic, blocking the road, preventing anyone else from going by.

When the sperm wants to move and does not, then it is as if the earth were not made for me at all, and I cannot walk with the cricket voyaging over his Gobi of wood chips; he is too free for me. I hear a howling in the air.

And what the soul offers, we never see clearly, though the spears fly through the air, crossing above our heads . . . and the naked old man walks by the ecstatically grieving sea, by the tumbling waters. . . . And how can the soul walk without its body? When its own seed stops the wheel, then the body lets nothing through its pores, it longs to groan and stretch out, to walk in procession shaking the sistrum, to disappear into the fog. . . .

And it is knotted. The sun hunches over and walks with its eyes on the ground, the moon hardens, it will not pass away, it refuses to become the sickle, but holds up its face at the window. . . . The water goes back disappointed to the root, the house of sticks falls, we stand alone on the plain. . . .

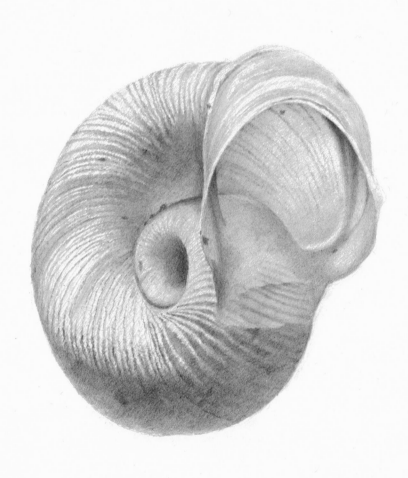

The Pail

Friend, this body is made of camphor and gopherwood. So
for two days I gathered ecstasies from my own body, I rose
up and down, surrounded only by bare wood and bare air
and some gray cloud, and what was inside me came so close
to me, and I lived and died!

Now it is morning. The faint rain of March hits the bark of
the half-grown trees. The honeysuckle will drip water, the
moon will grow wet sailing, the granary door turns dark on
the outside, the oats inside still dry.

And the grandfather comes back inquiringly to the farm,
his son stares down at the pickup tire, the family lawyer loses
his sense of incompetence for a moment, in the barn the big
pail is swung out so as to miss the post.

Snow Falling on Snow

Snow has fallen on snow for two days behind the Keilen farmhouse . . . no one has walked through it, or looked at it. . . . It makes the sound the porgies hear near the ocean floor, the sound the racer hears before his death, the sound that lifts the buoyant swimmer in the channel.

Wind blows four pigeon-grass heads, scarce and fine, above the snow. They are heron legs in white morning fog, a musical thought that rises as the pianist sits down at her table, the body laboring before dawn to understand its dream. . . .

Everyone else in the house still asleep. . . . In its dream thin feet come down the mountainside, hooves clatter over the wooden bridges, walk along the stone walls, and then pause, and look in at an orchard, where a fount of water is rising in the air. . . . Men are lying asleep all around its base, each with his sword lying under him. And the orchard-keeper, where is he?

We Love This Body

My friend, this body is made of energy compacted and whirling. It is the wind that carries the henhouse down the road dancing, and an instant later lifts all four walls apart. It is the horny thumbnail of the retired railway baron, over which his children skate on Sunday, it is the forehead bone that does not rot, the woman priest's hair still fresh among Shang ritual things. . . .

We love this body as we love the day we first met the person who led us away from this world, as we love the gift we gave one morning on impulse, in a fraction of a second, that we still see every day, as we love the human face, fresh after love-making, more full of joy than a wagonload of hay.

Wings Folding Up

The cucumbers are thirsty, their big leaves turn away from
the wind. I water them after supper, the hose lies curled near
the rhubarb. The wind sound blows through the head, a
smile appears on the sitter's face as he sits down under a tree.
What is comforted words help, the sunken islands speak to
us. . . .

Is this world animal or vegetable? Others love us, the
cabbages love the earth, the earth is fond of the heavens—a
new age comes close through the dark, an elephant's trunk
waves in the darkness, so much is passing away, so many
disciplines already gone, but the energy in the double flower
does not falter, the wings fold up around the sitting man's
face. And these cucumber leaves are my body, and my thighs,
and my toes stretched out in the wind. . . . Well, waterer,
how will you get through this night without water?

Snowed In

It is the third day of snow. Power has been out since yesterday. The horses stay in the barn. At four I leave the house, sinking to my waist in snow, and push open the study door. Snow falls in. I sit down at the desk, there is a plant in blossom.

The upper petal is orange-red. The lower petal paler, as if the intensity had risen upward. Two smaller petals, like country boys' ears, poke out on either side.

The blossom faces the window where snow sweeps past at forty miles an hour. . . . So there are two tendernesses looking at each other, two oceans living at a level of instinct surer than mine . . . yet in them both there is the same receiving, the longing to be blown, to be shaken, to circle slowly upward, or sink down toward roots . . . one cold, one warm, but neither wants to go up geometrically floor after floor, even to hold up a wild-haired roof, with copper dragons, through whose tough nose rain water will pour. . . .

So the snow and the orangey blossoms are both the same flow, that starts out close to the soil, close to the floor, and needs no commandments, no civilization, no drawing rooms lifted on the labor of the claw hammer, but is at home when one or two are present, it is also inside the block of wood, and in the burnt bone that sketched the elk by smoky light.

A man and woman sit quietly near each other. In the snowstorm millions of years come close behind us, nothing is lost, nothing rejected, our bodies are equal to the snow in energy. The body is ready to sing all night, and be entered by whatever wishes to enter the human body singing. . . .

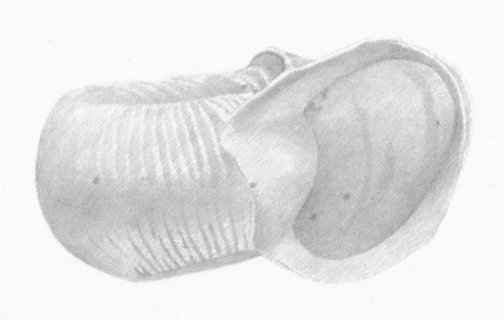

The Cry Going Out over Pastures

I love you so much with this curiously alive and lonely
body. It is a young hawk sitting on a tree by the Mississippi,
in early spring, before any green has appeared on the earth
beneath. I love you among my chest, where walnut hollows
fill with crackling light and shadows. . . . There birds drink
from water drops. . . . It loves you with what it extracts from
the prudent man, hunched over his colony of lizards, with
that it loves you madly, beyond all rules and conventions,
even the six holes in the flute move about under the dark
man's fingers, and the piercing cry goes out over the grown
up pastures no one sees or visits at dusk except the deer, out
of all enclosures, who has never seen any bed but his own of
wild grass.

I first met you when I had been alone for nine days, and
now my lonely hawk body longs to be with you, whom it
remembers . . . it knew how close we are, we would always
be. There is death but also this closeness, this joy when the
bee rises into the air above his hive to find the sun, to
become the son, and the traveler moves through exile and
loss, through murkiness and failure, to touch the earth again
of his own kingdom and kiss the ground. . . .

What shall I say of this? I say, praise to the first man who
wrote down this joy clearly, for we cannot remain in love
with what we cannot name. . . .

About the Artist

GENDRON JENSEN is a forest eccentric, who works in the often
neglected medium of the pencil. The drawings sometimes measure
five feet by six feet, and usually go in a series. He has completed a
series on the keybone plate of small turtles and a series that
includes the pod of the May apple and dragonfly wings, and a series
on the bones of a yearling deer. The snail series was created for
this book. He lives near Grand Rapids, Minnesota, and is
thirty-seven years old.

About the Author

ROBERT BLY has been working for several years in the often
neglected medium of the prose poem. He has written that we often
feel in a prose poem a man or woman talking not before a crowd,
but in a low voice to someone he is sure is listening. Through the
way the prose poem absorbs detail, it helps to heal the wound of
abstraction. He lives on a farm near Madison, Minnesota, spends
much time in the woods alone, and is fifty years old.